THE
Archive Photographs
SERIES

AROUND
LOUTH

The Southwold Hunt Boxing Day Meet at the Cattlemarket, c. 1955.

Front cover illustration: William Allison with a group of pupils from Louth's Free Evening School on what is now Louth Golf Course, c. 1870. The spire of St James's is visible in the distance.

THE
Archive Photographs
SERIES

AROUND LOUTH

Compiled by
David Cuppleditch

CHALFORD

First published 1995
Copyright © David Cuppleditch, 1995

The Chalford Publishing Company
St Mary's Mill, Chalford,
Stroud, Gloucestershire, GL6 8NX

ISBN 0 7524 0118 1

Typesetting and origination by
The Chalford Publishing Company
Printed in Great Britain by
Redwood Books, Trowbridge

Dedication
to Sally Hanford

Contents

Prizes of £40,000, £30,000, £20,000,
And 12,000 GUINEAS IN GOLD!

STATE LOTTERY BEGINS 19th JULY, 1815.

SCHEME.

A Prize of £30,000	3 .... of .. £20,000 are £60,000	**2,000 GUINEAS**
	3 .... 10,000 30,000	The 10 First-drawn Blanks, the 1st day, will each receive 200 Guineas in Gold, making
	1 .... 5,250 5,250	
	1 .... 2,000 2,000	The Fortieth-drawn Prize will receive in Addition
	3 .... 1,050 3,150	**5,000 GUINEAS**
	5 .... 30 5,000	
	4 .... 525 2,100	The 5th, 10th, and 15th drawn Blanks, the second day, will each receive 1,000 Guineas in Gold, making
	10 .... 210 2,100	
A Prize of £40,000	16 .... 100 1,600	
	26 .... 50 1,500	**3,000 GUINEAS**
	1,500 .... 15 22,500	
	1,500 Blanks 1st day 10 each 15,000	The 20th, 30th, 40th & 50th drawn Blanks, the third day, will each receive 500 Guineas in Gold, making
A Prize of £20,000	15,000 Tickets. £150,000	**2,000 GUINEAS**
	Price—Ticket £22 15 0	
	Half £11 14 0 Eighth £3 0 6	
	Fourth £ 9 0 Sixteenth £1 10 6	

I beg leave respectfully to solicit your attention to the Scheme of the present STATE LOTTERY, to begin drawing 19th JULY, which I venture to flatter myself, from the increased number and magnitude of the Prizes, and the unprecedented advantages it contains, will be honoured by an extraordinary degree of patronage and support. It will be found, on inspection to possess Two superb Prizes of £40,000, and £30,000, besides others of £20,000, &c. &c. &c. also Eighteen Golden Prizes, containing 12,000 GUINEAS, which will be Paid to the fortunate Purchasers, in GOLD, as soon as drawn, without any deduction

I trust that the consideration of these superlative benefits will induce you to become an adventurer in the present attractive Lottery, where the chances of gaining such important Prizes are greatly multiplied:—and any commands with which I may be honoured will be highly esteemed, and executed with the most prompt attention and punctuality.

I remain, very respectfully,

Your obedient Servant,

H. HURTON.

Louth, June, 1815.

TICKETS and SHARES are Selling by

H. HURTON,
Bookseller, LOUTH,

For RICHARDSON, GOODLUCK & Co. Contractors for the present Lottery, London.

State Lottery notice.

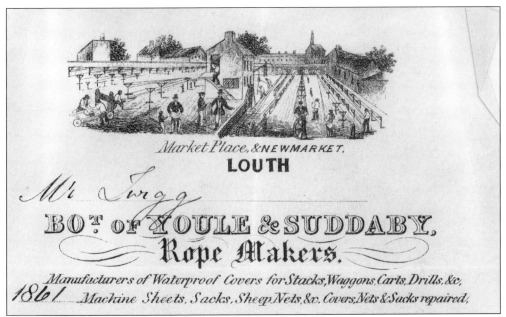

Before the days of photography firms and shopkeepers had to rely on illustration. This was Youle & Suddaby's Rope Works on Newmarket, which was still operating in the 1930s.

Introduction

Louth is a quiet Wolds market town with a friendly, cheerful and tolerant population. Its wealth has largely depended on farming and agriculture and one or two larger-than-life personalities have peppered its history and given the town its character. Sadly, too few present-day characters, inhabitants of our modern 'classless society', match up to their forebears.

It has been the same with photography. Despite all the leaps in technology, the photographs of Victorians Joseph Willey and Plumtree, or Edwardians Arthur and Clarence James, are often of a quality superior to their present-day counterparts. In this 'throwaway' society money is more important than quality. Maybe that's why the National Lottery is so popular; the whole country has developed gambling fever. But, in the last century, when J. Hurton issued tickets, everything eventually got out of hand and the State Lottery was abandoned. Let's hope our National Lottery will go the same way. Its almost as if people clutch at straws because everything around them has crumbled.

Witness the current interest in nostalgia and memorabilia. As people become disillusioned with local government, the Church and education, they look to the past to see what has gone wrong and to remember a time before it did. Since the Second World War local building policy has been characterized by haste and incompetence and the results are mundane. Each week brings fresh allegations in the lurid press of scandal among the clergy. And in education, the 'Mr Chips' of an earlier generation, teachers of some individuality who inhabited the fifties and sixties, have gone. Nowadays teachers abound, giving the impression that anyone thought incapable of achieving anything in life has automatically been given a teaching qualification! Just about every second person you meet in Louth is either a teacher or a retired teacher. And yet standards of literacy continue to decline.

There are far too few job opportunities for the young. Vandalism is not a modern problem. It was just as widespread in Victorian times as it is today – hence the shutters on shop windows and bolts on doors. Boredom and the lack of opportunity have always turned the young into hooligans. Perhaps Louth's rich selection of teachers could spend part of their third-of-a-year holiday on outward-bound courses or vocational studies; Louth's youth would benefit greatly!

During this century many famous names have enjoyed the town's hospitality, including Gandhi, who visited the town twice. T.E. Lawrence stopped for petrol for his motorbike when he was staying *incognito* as Aircraftsman Ross on Steep Hill, Lincoln. Lloyd George was pelted by some over-zealous suffragettes and Stanley Baldwin played a flying visit en route to Hainton Hall. More recently, that wonderful character, actor James Robertson Justice stopped off in Louth while visiting a falconry in Horncastle, and Enoch Powell attended a service in St James when visiting relatives in Ludborough. John Betjeman visited Louth many times, always staying with his old college mate, Jack Yates. Betjeman admired the graceful lines of St James' church spire but detested the over-indulgence of the Cornmarket's old frontage. It was Betjeman, in conjunction with Henry Thorold, who influenced John Piper to become interested in Lincolnshire's rich selection of parish churches. Even more recently the singer Barbara Dickson has made her home near Louth.

Of the many publications on Louth, *Notitae Ludae* (published in 1834) is probably the most comprehensive. There have been many other books since, including Harold Jackson's fun publications produced mainly for charity. But the most amazing facts are hidden among the stories which reach the local newspapers, many of which are unprintable containing as they do lurid aspects of town life. If Dylan Thomas were ever to be reincarnated and visit Louth he would have a field day.

One
Victorian and
Edwardian Louth

The earliest photographer working in Louth was Joseph Willey of 7 Aswell Lane. The carte-de-visite on the left, an example of his work, shows a Victorian lady nervously holding a letter. The photograph of Joseph Willey on the right was probably taken by his brother.

Another early Louth photographer was Plumtree, of The Studio, Ramsgate.

Plumtree's view of louth from the Cemetery, showing the old stables in the foreground.

Plumtree specialised in street scenes and landscapes. This was the view looking up Chequergate.

Probably the most prolofic of Ludensian photographers was A. James of Ramsgate House. These cartes-de-visite capture a young girl clutching a doll and a distinguished old farming type.

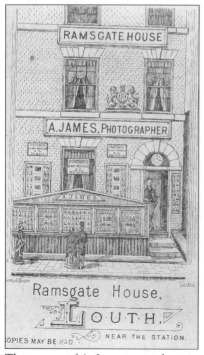
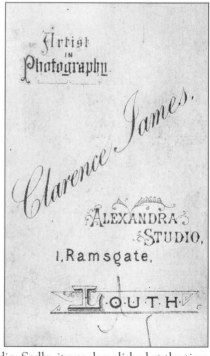

The reverse of A. James carte-de-visite, showing his studio. Sadly, it was demolished at the time of the Louth flood. The other Edwardian photographer was Clarence James of Alexandra Studio, 1 Ramsgate. This was latterly used by Clare photographers.

The young girl in this Clarence James portrait shot has a handsome bustle and trim figure.

Louth's most important asset, next to St James's church, is undoubtedly Hubbard's Hills, a favourite family haunt even in Edwardian times.

This pre-First World War postcard shows Hubbard's Hills as it was. Initially this was known as Hubbard's Valley.

Two girls sporting boaters and navy blue dresses have to keep very still.

An even earlier photograph shows that the Hills have changed little over the years.

Many Edwardian families sat eagerly for their portrait shot. This shows the Pridmore family, whose tailoring business still operates in Eastgate.

15

Victorian group shots were also popular. This shows the Ashley and Sons Iron Works staff, who operated off Ashley Lane. The cinders from this firm's furnaces gave Cinder Lane its name, while the name of the firm is remembered in Ashley Road.

Even in this photograph of the Priory there are two Victorian men posing casually against the wall.

Curiosity about the magic box brought many people out into the street, such as in this view of Eastgate.

Louth was particularly proud of its Grammar School. This shows a group of boys assembled outside the Lodge. Old boys included Alfred Lord Tennyson, Captain John Smith and Sir John Franklin.

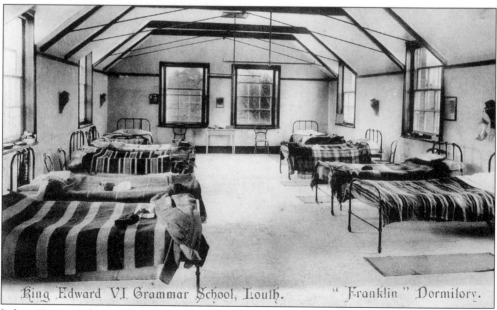

King Edward VI Grammar School, Louth.   "Franklin" Dormitory.

Life was spartan during Tennyson's time, and from this photograph of 'Franklin's Dormitory' it would seem that conditions had not changed much by the turn of the century.

One of the most prized Grammar School possessions is the bust of Captain John Smith (the founder of Virginia, who was saved by Pocahontas), which was made by Baden-Powell and presented to the school in 1907.

Below, left: Of all the old Grammar School Ludensians, none was to benefit the town more than Richard William Goulding (1868-1929). A scholar and historian by profession, Goulding was responsible for founding the Louth Naturalists Club in 1884, later known as the Louth Naturalists Antiquarian and Literary Society (Ants & Nats). His collection of books and ephemera has proved invaluable to historians. This unique collection was presented to the Louth Library after his death by the Duchess of Portland and is currently housed in Northgate.

Below, right: This was Richard Goulding's unpretentious home, No. 26 Gospelgate, currently owned by pop star 'Jilted John' (Graham Fellows).

Following Richard Goulding's death his sisters Annie (left) and Gertrude (right), who lived next door at 28 Gospelgate, continued with the family business of book printing and bookselling from Goulding's bow-fronted shop in Mercer Row.

An early Grammar School football team.

King Edward VI Grammar School, Louth.   The Dining Hall.

The Dining Hall, where the boys were forced to sit at long trestle tables and juggle on uncomfortable benches.

For outdoor exercise there was the Long Pen. Boys were also encouraged to take cold showers.

The Girls Grammar School opened in James Street in 1903. This shows a group of thirteen of the original fourteen pupils who formed the first girls Grammar School in Lindsey. In 1904 trustees from the Pahud Estate presented Lindsey House for the use of the Girls' Grammar School.

22

King Edward VI Girls' Grammar School,
Louth, Lincs. Assembly Hall.

Boys and girls were strictly segregated. This shows the interior of the Girls' Assembly Hall.

LOUTH, LINCOLNSHIRE,

*Superior Residence for a Gentleman of independent fortune,
or engaged in either of the professions.*

TO BE SOLD BY PRIVATE CONTRACT.

The Girls' Grammar School soon established itself as a force to be reckoned with, on account of the discipline of Miss Masson, Miss Nalder and, later, Miss Hardy. A school magazine printed by Gouldings was produced with the school motto 'E Pluribus unum'.

Before being admitted to Louth Grammar School, local girls and boys had the choice of the National School in Westgate or the British School in Kidgate. Here we see Mr Trewick, headmaster of Kidgate, and some pupils from the last century.

One of the highlights of the school year was the dance around the Maypole, which was performed in Westgate Fields. Mr Trewick is in charge.

At one time Louth enjoyed a good railway system. Thorn's coaches taxied parties to and from Louth Station. Mr Thorn is the gentleman standing in the centre with a silver beard.

Louth came under the old borough system. This photograph, the only one known to exist, shows all the councillors in the one shot. It was taken at the opening of Alvingham Waterworks, *c.* 1908.

Louth Cattlemarket enjoyed a bustling trade, and for many farmers this was the hub of their existence.

As the popularity of the cattlemarket increased new pens were added.

The most prestigious store in Louth was Eve and Ranshaws. Founded in 1781, the firm's name reflected the various partners until 1876, when it became Eve and Ranshaw. The firm still thrives today under the ownership of the Sandwith family, who bought it in 1977.

They undertook deliveries as well as removals. This shows their van going up Horncastle Road, with South Street House (now known as The Beeches Nursing Home) in the background.

There was plenty of work for scullery maids.

This cook worked for the Broadley family and the photograph was taken outside their house at the top of Lee Street. This house may be seen on the left of the white hut on both of the pictures on page 26.

The view looking down Mercer Row. Gas lamps lit up dark winter evenings.

George Street, with the 'Tower House' on the right. It is said that the tower was built for a merchant to view his ships as they came up the canal.

Grimsby Road has changed considerably, many buildings having been demolished and new dwellings put in their place.

The old Cornmarket has also vanished. John Betjeman never liked it, but I rather think he would have liked the mundane frontage of the Halifax Building Society erected in its place even less.

It is easy to see from this postcard why the old Cornmarket suffered its fate. The frontage was just a fascia and the stones were laid the wrong way round which led to weathering. The stones crumbled and the building was eventually considered unsafe.

Louth's fire engine. Prior to the First World War it served the town well.

Most families enjoyed a comfortable yet strict regime. This shows Mrs Surgery, wife of the Vicar of Muckton, with her sons Monty and Gordon.

There were many chapels in the town. This was the Free Methodist's Chapel in Eastgate next door to the Woodman Inn. It was demolished in the early '60s because the pillars were considered unsafe; the site was used as a car park.

Two
Between the Wars

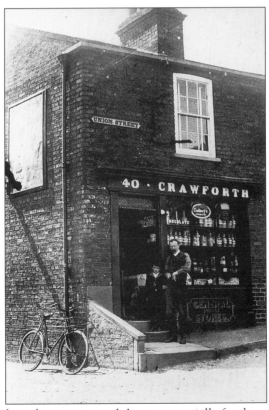

Life was tough in Louth in the twenties and thirties, especially for those with small businesses. This shows Crawforth's grocery shop in Union Street.

There was always work for cobblers such as Edwin Day who kep this boot and shoe shop on the corner of Eve Street and Northgate. reverse photo

This photograph shows clearly where Edwin Day's shop was in relation to Albert Horsewood's furniture shop. It has since been demolished and is currently a recreational area.

This photograph of a march past on Memorial Sunday suggests why cobblers were kept so busy: most people had to walk when Louth had little motor traffic.

Most transport was horse-driven, and horses, like humans, needed attention. The last blacksmith in Louth was A. Dunkin of Eve Street, who came to Louth in 1909 and retired in 1961.

Louth has always possessed an excellent range of butchers. This was Gurbutt's poultry shop in the Cornmarket, on the site of what is now Philip Stevens estate agents office.

Every Christmas turkeys were displayed in profusion. It is interesting to note that chicken was considered a delicacy at this time. But this was before battery farming.

Louth was noted for manufacturing Luda bicycles, pens, carpets, soap, wallpaper and bottles. Luda toffee was made by Strawson's.

Louth was always on the lookout for new modes of transport such as these early types of moped. Ludensian Otto Mayer, born in 1866, was responsible for pioneering the first petrol motor engines. In 1885 he left Louth for the Gottlieb Daimler workshop near Stuttgart, where he assisted with the first Benz engines.

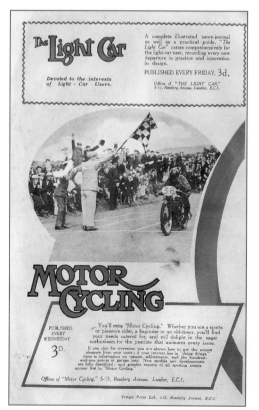

Interest in motor-driven traffic led to the setting up of Cadwell Vale motor cycle track near Louth. Now Cadwell Park, this was formerly the home of the Allenby family. Early enthusiasts for the sport included J. Beeton of Louth and F. Frith of Grimsby.

Travel by omnibus or charanbanc was often uncomfortable. This was Banana Bob's travelling van.

Banana Bob established a good reputation in Louth and his bus was traded for a market stall. He was long remembered for his patch on the Fish Shambles.

Other provision dealers took note of this; Holborn's travelling van took goods from door to door.

Depsite all the competition Larder's grocery store still thrived. Here we see it decorated for the 1935 celebrations of King George V's Silver Jubilee. It has not fared quite so well in recent times with the advent of all the supermarkets and has had to remove into smaller premises just off Mercer Row.

Onet casualty was Burton's tailoring shop in Mercer Row. 'Gone for a Burton' might have been an apposite comment!

What is so fascinating about the twenties and thirties are the fashions. This dashing man-about-town with his demure escort is none other than Neville Spencer, son of a coal merchant; he was later to open a successful newsagents in Louth.

One of the main differences between then and now was headgear. Even when St James choir went on their annual outing all the men wore hats or caps. Owen Price, the organ master, is in the centre of the group, fourth from the left.

Tennis fashions have changed beyond all recognition, as can be seen by these two Louth Grammar School girls photographed on Julian Bower.

This photograph of Monks Dyke School, which opened in 1929, features quite an array of twenties dresses and the odd cloche hat.

Many a Ludensian seamstress was put to the test when it came to the annual children's fancy dress ball held either in Louth Town Hall or the old Liberal Club. These costumes were mostly home-made and showed considerable flair.

Some costumes had an unabashed patriotic fervour which is in complete contrast to modern attitudes.

Public subscription paid for Louth's new fire engine, photographed here on the London Road football pitch.

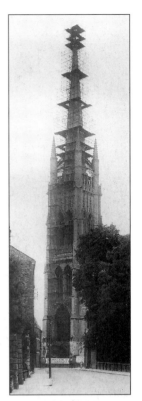

The other great task in the thirties was the restoration of St James's spire. A service of Thanksgiving was held in St James on Sunday 24 1938.

The big event in the thirties was the Silver Jubilee celebrations of George V and Mary, when practically the entire town turned out to enjoy the festivities.

A special children's party was held in the old roller-skating rink in Ramsgate (now occupied by Hi-Lite signs). It was an attempt to lift morale following the years of Depression.

The best recorded event in the early part of the century was a tragedy. The Louth flood of 1920 was sparked off by freak rainfall in the Wolds. The ensuing wall of water hit Louth after 5 p.m. on 29 May and caused havoc. A train was running along the old Withcall line as the waters descended on the town.

The torrent of water passes through Withcall on its way down to the River Lud.

It hit the bridge at the bottom of the Grimsby road and practically demolished it.

Spout Yard, Turpins Yard (James Street) and Ramsgate were particularly badly hit. This shows Ramsgate.

Afterwards it was a question of clearing up the mess.

Many people in Bridge Street lost personal possessions, though most felt they had been lucky to escape with their lives.

In 1926 the World Ploughing Championships were held at Boswell near Louth. The overall winner was Mr Jacklin, whose son still lives in Louth.

At one time there were at least three brickyards in Louth. Mr Darnill's, off Charles Street, close to where this photograph was taken, was demolished in the 1920 flood.

Another was MacDougal's brickyard off Priory Row, in between Monks Dyke Road and Eastgate. It was used as a builders merchants yard before the houses of Priory Close were erected on this site.

Les Howe (1897-1959), seen here sitting on an old wooden bench in Hubbards Hills, was one of the many Louth photographers.

He was a frequent visitor to Bateman's old swimming pool in Maiden Row. The water was usually freezing!

An annual feature in Louth was the Hospital Cup Final, which raised money for the Crowtree Lane District Hospital and provided soccer enthusiasts in the twenties with some enjoyment.

The game was as competitive in 1924 as it is today, although the shorts have changed.

KING EDWARD VI GR

The Girls' Grammar School in 1927, when Miss Nalder was headmistress.

AR SCHOOL FOR GIRLS,

The emergence of the Louth Playgoers in 1932 gave us some lively performances. Many of the early stars, such as F. Harness, who acted in the 1931 version of *Miss Hook of Holland*, were from the Louth Operatic Society.

T. Foster played the Emperor in the 1933 production of *San Toy*.

Arthur Price (son of organist Owen Price) was Jack Point in 1934. A young dapper Jimmy Wilson appeared in 1937.

One of the heart throbs of the Louth Operatic Society was John Harrison, who appeared in the 1938 version of *Hit the Deck*.

Margaret Godsmark was often leading lady. Here we see her in the 1933 version of *San Toy*.

Mr Hemming was another stalwart. He appeared in the 1931 version of *Miss Hook of Holland* as Schnapps.

Louth Amateur Operatic Society.

1935.

The **DESERT SONG**

GILZA DESIGN.
COPYRIGHT, P.B.& M—B.

Souvenir Programme   *Price 6d. each.*

J. Harrison was the Red Shadow in this 1935 production of *Desert Song*, playing opposite Margaret Godsmark as Margot.

One of the more unusual houses in Louth is Abbey House, the converted farmhouse and long time home of the Dixon family. It is now in the hands of the Tebbs family and the ruins of Louth Park Abbey are in the back garden.

This unusual Japanese bridge is also within the grounds. Built in the sixties by Architect Houfe, it serves as a special feature of the house.

In the back garden of Abbey House is the ruin of the old Cistercian Louth Park Abbey. This photograph was taken at the turn of the century, shortly after Allison's archeological dig.

Kenwick Hall was another fine house. One time the home of the Allenby family, then the Garfits, and latterly Diana Dixon, it is now a private golf club.

A Second World War bomb made the structure of Kenwick Hall unsafe. It was subsequently pulled down and the present hall built.

The front lodge to Kenwick Hall has changed little.

Stewton House was built in 1750. In 1927 it was completely rebuilt and was for many years after the home of the Sutcliffe family. In 1952 it opened as a home for the elderly, and it is currently a private nursing home run by Mr and Mrs Ewing.

The Temperance Society set out to tackle Victorian and Edwardian Louth's drink problem. The old Temperance Hotel was eventually demolished in the sixties to make way for a supermarket and the Temperance Society gave up.

Louth Volunteers eventually became Louth Rifle Club. This group pictured in the fifties comprised, back row, left to right: Charlie Lane, Mr Hill, Billy Platt, Major Boswell, Mrs Boswell, Bill Richardson, Mrs Paulson. Front row: Mr Laking and Michael Mawer.

Three
Loweth's Hostelries

The oldest surviving pub in Louth is Ye Olde Whyte Swanne, sometimes nicknamed 'The Mucky Duck'. It was referred to in 1612 as the 'Sign of the Swans'. Next to it was the Marquis of Granby, demolished to make way for the town hall car park.

The new library in Northgate was built on the site of the Pack Horse Tap.

The present Golden Fleece was built in the yard of the old Golden Fleece Hotel.

The Brown Cow at the top of Church Street has become the Newmarket Inn. Run by the Smith family, who have renovated what was an old spit-and-sawdust dive frequented by farmers and labourers on market day, it now enjoys a new lease of life.

A group of locals dressed as yokels photographed at the back of The Woodman in Eastgate in the thirties or forties. In 1850 the landlord here was a William King.

The Old Ship and Horns on the corner of the Fish Shambles was known by several names. In 1782 it was known as the Royal Sovereign and in 1791 the Royal George. It did not acquire its present name until 1850.

The Woolpack down by the Riverhead has only changed inasmuch as it used to be called the Wool Pack. The name probably derived from the bales of wool which were shipped down the canal.

The Brown Horse in Queens Street was once a favorite haunt of airmen from RAF Manby. Before becoming a pub it was a joiners yard belonging to Harrison's the builders. Empty bar stools now line the saloon, a reminder of this once bustling hostelry.

Just round the corner in Maiden Row was The Three Magpies, run for years by the Stamp family. When this terraced block was demolished to make way for Elizabeth Court the pub was demolished as well.

Another recently demolished pub is the George Hotel, which gives its name to George Street. It closed in 1904 and was used as a school before being turned into flats.

The Dutch-gabled building in Pawnshop Passage was once a pub known as the Golden Ball. Later it became a pawnshop, from which the name of Pawnshop Passage originated, having previously been called Hurton's Yard.

Another ancient pub was the Volunteer Arms in Northgate, named after the Old Louth Volunteers. In the distance is the Wilde Memorial Hall which was demolished to make way for Northgate Court.

One of Louth's newest hostelries is the Lady of Shallot, off Northolme Road, named after Tennyson's poem. This shows a Harvest Festival auction with the familiar figure of Matthew Grist on the extreme left.

The Greyhound in Upgate has undergone several changes of management in recent times. A marathon pool match is under way in the main bar.

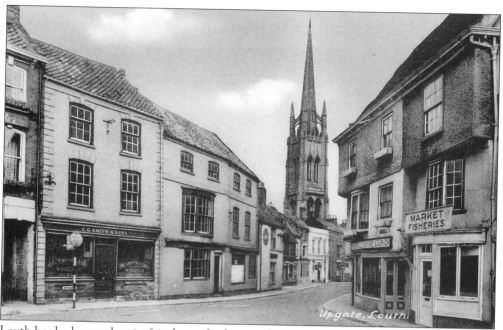

Louth has had more than its fair share of pubs over the years. In the 1950s, when the population was only around 9,000, there were about forty-eight pubs! This shows the old Blue Stone Tavern (on the left, next to C.G. Smith's office) and the old Black Bull two doors away which is now an opticians.

The Mason's Arms in the Cornmarket was first licensed in 1782 as the Bricklayers Arms. It became a posting house and for many years enjoyed the excellent patronage of local farmers.

A group of Old Ludensian worthies in the dining room of the Mason's Arms. Among those present are Mr Hunter, Cecil Simpson, George Hall, Mr Bach (senior), Bertie Hallam and, in the distance, a young Steve Lee. This group photograph, taken in the 1950s by Bert Rawlings, shows dinner being served on damask tablecloths with old-fashioned cutlery and waitresses in 'pinnies'.

The main rival to the Mason's Arms as a posting house was the King's Head, which opened in 1775.

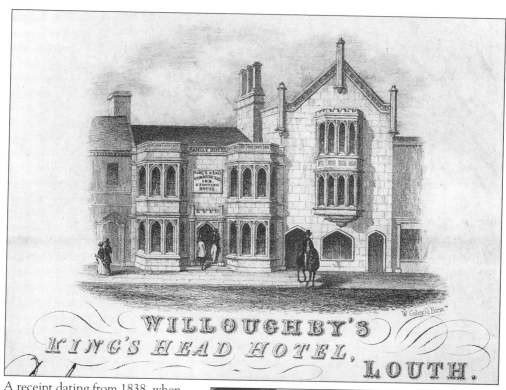

A receipt dating from 1838, when George Willoughby owned the New King's Head.

The front of the King's Head, Mercer Row, was suitably decorated for the festivities during the celebrations of 1935.

The Wheatsheaf in Westgate was the watering-hole for farm labourers delivering their carts of corn. In 1850, Thomas Clapham was brewing his own beer, which he called 'Wheat Sheaf' brew.

In the 1920s and '30s charabancs became popular. This party set off from the rear of the White Hart in Aswell Street (now demolished). At one time the White Hart was known as the Blackmoor's Head.

Even in this photograph there is a pub, The Shades, on the left of the steps. The name was derived from the shades of a windmill. Today the site is occupied by Barclays Bank.

One of the reasons that alcohol was so popular in Louth was that the town housed two local breweries, one in the vicinity of Uncle Tom's Cabin and the other on a site off New Street. The New Street brewery had a network of tunnels leading to many local hostelries in and around the Cornmarket, such as the Crown and Woolpack (now Victoria Wine) on the corner of Cornmarket and New Street.

Because of the local breweries, there was a demand for hops. This was Ryley's warehouse at the bottom of Aswell Street (now known as the Maltings).

Louth's newest pub, the Lincolnshire Poacher, was at one time called Park House. During the Second World War it was the headquarters for numerous regiments, and Churchill once stayed overnight here. It was formerly the home of Charles William Tindall (1849-1926), who founded the Lincoln Red Cattle Society.

Four
Louth in the 1950s

In 1947 Britain was gripped by a vicious winter. These were the snow drifts on the London Road in Louth.

The town was completely cut off and there was little to do except bring out the sledges and enjoy some winter sports!

One casualty during the Second World War was the malt kiln on Newbridge Hill. Its replacement not only gave Louth the largest malt silo in Europe, but also a blot that has plagued Louth ever since. (Photograph H.L. Howe)

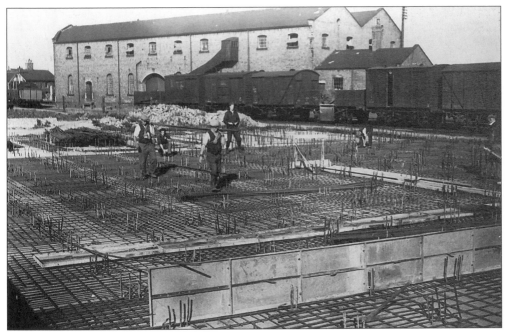

The malt kiln was so large because of war-aid compensation. The new kiln had to be built on exactly the same site as the old one. (Photograph H.L. Howe)

Most people tried to resume a normal lifestyle after the turbulent war years. This was the cast of the Louth Playgoers' version of *Pink String and Sealing Wax*, produced in 1948.

This shows Barton's orchestra, appearing for a St Michael's garden fête. They are, from left to right: Cyril Coxon, Colin Brown, George Borman, Lance Brown, Bert Croft, Reg Smith, Albert Stanley, Maxwell Goodwin, Walter Barton and Tom Rawdon.

Another group who formed a band were the 'Rhythm Rocketeers', seen here in the Town Hall, On the right, with the saxophone and bow tie, was Basil Lock, who later became an Air Vice-Marshal in the RAF and who, incidentally, taught the Duke of Edinburgh to fly.

Few people in Louth have done quite so much for charity as Phyllis West. This early photograph of her (second from left) was taken in the early 1950s at a soirée. Also present are Mrs Eve, Mrs Herbert and Mrs Neave.

There was much emphasis on housing during the post-war years. This was the Housing Committee in a new bungalow off Stewton Lane. (Photograph Bert Rawlings)

There were also numerous presentations in the 1950s, such as this bowls weather vane, which was presented to Harold Drinkel (right) by John Barker (left), the Borough Surveyor.

Another presentation was this wallplate clock given to Mr Robinson (left) by Jack Yates, then the president of the Louth Ants and Nats.

In 1955 the Grenadier Guards visited Louth to recruit potential guardsmen. A ball was held in the Town Hall to mark the event.

In November 1955 there was a tramp supper held in Stewton Lane, which shows that Ludensians could produce an imaginative selection of costumes.

During the 1950s sport was taken seriously. At the Sportsmen's Week Dinner of 1954 there was a vast array of trophies. Behind them are the familiar faces of Roberts, F. Macdonald, H. Drinkel, H.O. Smith, and Mayor William Robert Burr. (Photograph Bert Rawlings)

In 1955 the Sportsmen's Week Dinner held in the Town Hall was over-subscribed.

Monks Dyke School had proved such a success that a further school was needed. In 1954 the tractors went onto the waste ground between North Holme Road and High Holme Road to clear the way for Cordeaux School.

This was Lacey Gardens Junior School in the mid-1950s. The school, like Lacey Gardens itself, was named after Alderman Lacey, one-time Mayor of Louth.

Another Ludensian school, and one which receives little press, is St Michael's School. This photograph of a party was taken in the late 1950s or early 1960s.

During the 1950s Louth possessed the *North Lincolnshire and Louth Advertiser*. This photograph showed that newspapers employed a large staff compared to the skeleton crew employed today. The photograph was taken in Hanson's old café on Upgate.

There were always parties being held in Louth, such as this Mount Pleasant Christmas party in 1955 …

… and the Lincolnshire Road Car Dinner held in the Town Hall in 1953.

Mayor's Sunday, 1955. This was the procession going down Little Eastgate just ouside the now demolished Marquis of Granby. Albert Ernest Maxey was five times Mayor of Louth. He was a freeman of Louth, and is remembered in Maxey Court. In the background is Cyril Osborne, long time M.P. for Louth.

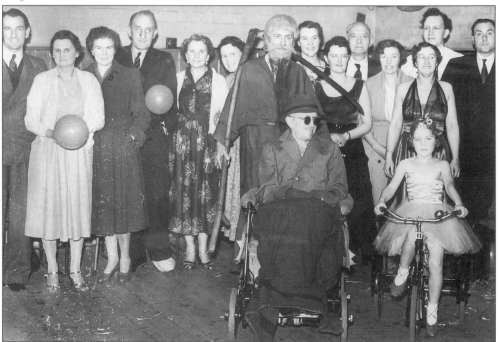

This was the New Year's Eve Dance in the Town Hall of 1956. The photograph was taken downstairs in the area of the old cells.

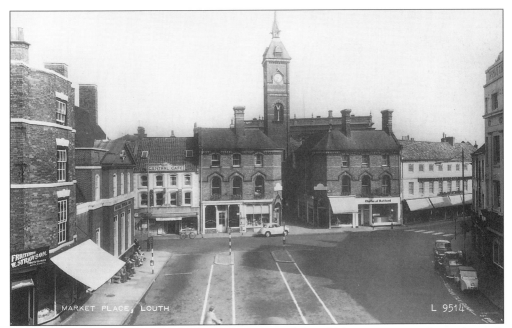

This picture of the Market Place shows that most of the old business names have changed. Strawson's fruit business, the Central Café, MacLeods, Clarks of Retford and Cheers and Parkers have gone. Even the old National Provincial has changed its name to the Nat West, but Eve and Ranshaw's store remains.

Sadly, in the post-war years many large country houses became unfashionable and were demolished. One of the victims was Walmsgate Hall, near Louth, formerly the home of the Dallas-Yorke family and noted for its splendid Italian gardens.

Since the Second World War, one of the most prolific Ludensian photographers has been Ken Atterby (above, now retired) who occasionally worked for the *Louth Standard* and who produced numerous postcards of Louth and the surrounding area. A close friend of Atterby's was Lenton Ottaway, whose shop (right) was just around the corner in Little Eastgate.

His studio in Northgate has since been converted into living accommodation.

Five
Modern Louth

Continuing the tradition of laying a wreath on Remembrance Sunday (1991) is Mayor Dorothy Grant with many familiar faces in the background. Most notable is Jill Makinson Saunders, whose vitriolic editorials are a feature of the *Louth Leader*.

The Old Mayor's Sunday Parade has diminished somewhat in recent times. Pictured are Mayor Roy Gathercole, followed by Dorothy Grant, Stan Ward, Mrs Munslow, Jack Wynn, and the town clerk, Fred Weir.

No book on Louth would be complete without the familiar face of John Lill, author of the *Louth Playgoers – the first sixty years*, a history of Louth's thriving amateur dramatic society. Here we see him between two scantily dressed starlets.

Another popular character about town, also among a bevy of beauties, is Peter Mountain, the estate agent, when he was Chairman of the Round Table.

One character who supported most of the hostelries in Louth was the late Jimmy Hines. Occasionally he would enter a pub looking as if he had just parked Concorde in the car park. From the amount of braid on his uniform it might have come as a surprise to find he was only the chief steward.

Many popular television personalities have visited Louth in recent times, including Dana, the Irish singer.

Peter Beale, from *Eastenders*, did not receive a very enthusiastic reception. Only three people and one dog turned up to meet this soap star at the Town Hall.

Seth Armstrong from *Emmerdale Farm* came to demonstrate Westwood lawnmowers.

Philip Schofield brought the Radio One Roadshow to Louth.

Recently removed from Louth is Karen Archer, who lived in Upgate with her actor husband David Collings. She is seen here (extreme right) raising money for the Rumanian Appeal.

Louth has many societies. Here we see Louth Bowls Club pictured outside their clubhouse just off St Mary's Lane. Sadly, many of these faces are no longer with us.

The present Male Voice Choir was formed in 1973 and enjoys strong links with 'Albatros' from Pekela in Holland. There have been four visits by the Louth Voice Choir to Holland since 1979, and 'Albatros' have also visited Louth on several occasions. (Photograph Ken Atterby)

The other great influence on Louth's musical talent has been Peter Burness, pictured here with his friend Peter Butters, who was choirmaster of St James. The noble spire of St James is in the background.

Another thriving club is Louth Athletic Club, who organize an annual race through the town.

For the discerning there is John Taylor's monthly antique sale. Organised by Ann Laverack and held in The Woolmart, this popular event has attracted buyers from all over the country.

On the night of 2 June 1991 a catastophe struck Holy Trinity Church, when it caught fire. The alarm was raised at 4 a.m. by John Yendell, who lived just opposite the church.

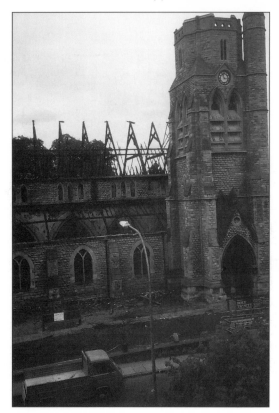

Within a short space of time, flames had engulfed the entire nave and chancel, leaving the church gutted. The damage, which was caused by an electrical fault, was so extensive that the remaining timber and walls had to be demolished, leaving only the tower and spire standing.

Another important event in Louth in June of the same year was the opening of Louth's long-awaited by-pass, which was officially celebrated on the 30th.

Nearly everyone in Louth turned out to watch the carnival which was organised by Louth Rotary Club. The programme included a display of vintage vehicles.

Here we see Edward Leigh MP, addressing a group of local Conservatives in Ayscough Hall, Lee Street. Leigh was reputedly the inspiration for Rick Mayall's character of A. B'astard in the popular television series *The New Statesman*.

An earlier Louth MP, Jeffrey Archer, went on to achieve fame as a popular novelist.

It was Peter Tapsell (now Sir Peter) who secured the Tory seat in Louth, succeeding Michael Brotherton.

This familiar view of Louth's Wednesday market, with Mr Thompson, the auctioneer of Broadgate & Thompson, taking charge of the proceedings, has altered little since the Second World War.

There is always something happening in Louth. Here, it is a teddy bears' picnic in Hubbard's Hills sponsored by Louth Lions.

An appeal for Help the Aged in 1987, when Roy Gathercole was Mayor.

At nearly every event where there is likely to be an accident St John Ambulance is present to administer first aid.

In 1987 the Duchess of Gloucester visited Louth.

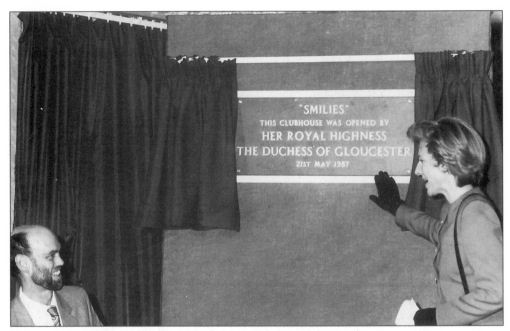

She was invited to open 'Smilies' Clubhouse, off St Bernard's Avenue.

In 1989 the Princess Royal opened Louth Livestock Centre on the Cattle Market. She was greeted by Mayor John Macdonald.

There was an unusually high attendance of farmers on that day!

One of the more recent groups, with a healthy membership of approximately 200 members, is Louth & District Flower Lovers. Started in the 1950s by stalwarts such as Mrs Fenwick, Mrs Harniess and Mrs Luty, it raises funds for many charities. Here we see a typical display in St James church, with Sybil Blossom and the verger Colin Crust looking on.

Louth has always had a keen interest in darts. This was a presentation of prizes at the Wellington Pub in 1979. (Photograph Ken Atterby)

One of the most familiar characters to be seen walking around Louth picking up litter and closing people's front gates is Ken Laking, seen here with his white stick and cloth cap and standing in front of Macdonald's traction engine.

On the industrial front, few people have brought more employment to the town than the late C.K. Addison. This photograph taken in 1978 has the familiar bulldog face of Mr Riddick, the then town clerk, in the background. (Photograph Ken Atterby)

A visit by Father Christmas to Bridge House Nursery School's Christmas party in 1978. (Photograph Ken Atterby)

The Southwold Hunt still meets at the Cattle Market every Boxing Day.

This remained a popular event …

… until the anti-hunt protesters moved in.

In 1985 there was a festival in Louth and one of the chief attractions was this group of Morris dancers.

Cadwell seems to gain increasing popularity each year. In 1976 Prince Michael of Kent, the late James Hunt, Barry Sheene, and Roger Clark all visited Cadwell Park.

One of the most popular local figures was eleven times British champion Roger Marshall, seen here presenting a cricket trophy in Horncastle to Brian Castle of the Ludensian firm Seymour & Castle.

Louth's own Red Cross Centre was opened as late as 25 February 1995. Situated in Pawnshop Passage under the guidance of Mayor Clive Finch, its opening marked 125 years of the British Red Cross.

Just as one centre opens, another part of Louth is destroyed. This photograph shows the old shops at the end of Church Street (at the junction with Eastgate) under the bulldozer's hammer. Was this demolition firm really called Muckshift or was it just a send-up?

Louth has always had a good selection of butchers. Here is Mr Laking (on the left) of Laking's Butchers with Malcolm Neal of Lloyds Bank presenting a cup for the best cow in the show.

Another popular butcher is Paul Matthews (right), showing off his prize sausages with Chris Fenwick.

Nostalgia is definitely back with a swing. This celebration of VE Day (sponsored by Louth's own Spire Radio) was held in the Town Hall.

Showing that Louth curios and antiquities are just as important as ever they were is Jean Howard, curator of Louth Museum, showing off the old station clock. Louth might not have a railway station any longer but at least it retains the clock.

There is even a Louth–Grimsby Railway Preservation Society which is trying to put back the old line. Alas, I fear it is too late.

Bob Oaks, the Alvingham blacksmith. This photograph makes clear that these pictures will one day have a great significance. It is not just the antique centre (advertised at the bottom) but also the individual antique hanging baskets that will in days to come be looked on as nostalgic memorabilia.

Over the years many sporting stars have visited Louth, including Geoff Capes, Rory Underwood, and more recently Peter Elliott, the 800 metres champion. It was a special treat for the students of Cordeaux when he visited the school and signed a few autographs.

This scene has been a familiar one in Louth for years: the 'Wednesday Cornmarket Auction'. Even in the short space of time since this photograph was taken by Geoffrey Dyon, the LSG and Mad Harry's shops have all gone.

Another school which is rarely mentioned is Deighton Close School, which deals with disturbed children (or children with disturbed parents, depending on your point of view). This photograph was taken when the school received a 'Schools Curriculum Award'.

Louth Lions, Rotary and Round Table all donate to charity every year. In this photograph Martin Chatterton is presenting the Lincolnshire Rural Activities Centre with a cheque for £750. At the latest count there are twelve charity shops in Louth. Nor does it end there. So many people are involved with charity work – from the arts, to Harold Jackson's publications, to sponsored sporting activities, Louth gives more than its fair share to charity.

Ladies on the move! Louth Library leaves its rented premies in Upgate to go to its new home in Newgate.

In an attempt to show that Louth is not a cultural desert, Charles Baron organised a Louth Festival in 1992. It was repeated two years later, and the grand Festival Ball, held in the Town Hall, had many supporters. In this photograph are the familiar faces of Messrs Griffiths, O'Malley, Haxby and, to the right, Margaret Ottaway with Rector Stephen Holdaway.

An unusual musical combination providing entertainment. From left to right: Neil Sharpley (the Louth Coroner), Paddy McCree, and Jayne Goldsmith. When last interviewed, Neil Sharpley was compiling a tome on what *not* to do on a coroner's table.

Of the many dance groups in Louth, one of the most unusual is this one organised by 'Lollipop' Jacqui Lidgard-Brown.

Louth has suffered one or two fires over the years. This one took place in Upgate in the eighties. In the foreground is builder Brian Smith.

Does this photograph show a past era? Sir Peter Tapsell and Lady Gabrielle with a portrait of Prime Minister John Major, under the guidance of Mayor John Deane. The photograph was taken in the Town and Country Club with the familiar face of Phyllis West next to Sir Peter.

Like the Lud which flows through Louth, so our present society will also disappear one day, leaving the noble spire of St James. If only the spire could tell tales! I wonder what it would come up with? This unusual view of St James with the Lud in the foreground is from the Mill House, Bridge Street.

Acknowledgements

For their assistance in putting this volume together I would like to thank the late James Baildom, Charles Smith, the late Harold Smith, Peter Craig, Peter Moore, Peter Chapman, Ben Jacklin, Stuart Ottaway and David Bryant.
A special thanks must go to the *Grimsby Evening Telegraph* for letting me reproduce one or two photographs in the latter part of this book, and indeed anyone else whom I may have inadvertantly forgotten.